Africa and Irregular Migration

by

Yaya Sillah

Also by the author

NON-FICTION

Marriage & Society

How to Build the Gambia (Attaining Economic Super-
power Status in Africa)

The Power of Positive Imagination

Why Do Good People Suffer?

How to Become a Millionaire

FICTION

Danjoo, A Miracle Child

We publish books in the pursuit of human advancement
Visit our website at www.subakunda.com
Email: subakunda@yahoo.com
Mobile: +2209459540
Address: Kotu West K.M.C, The Gambia

ISBN: 979-8710814703

Table of contents

Introduction

Over the past several years I have actively participated in various online discussions about issues regarding immigration and domestic politics and I have written extensively, both online and offline, to share my thoughts, in particular on The Gambia and West Africa. The feedback that I have received so far most people believe that my arguments are profoundly well-researched and compelling. I anthologise five articles here in this small book, "Africa and Irregular Migration".

1

The four categories of the SKP Migration Perception Index

a) Positive immigration

Traditionally known as the 'pull' factor in migration, we know it today as 'positive immigration'. This type of migration occurs when an individual sees business or employment opportunities arise elsewhere and has a huge expectation of earning more wealth in another country. A diverse range of businesses and skilled workers are incentivised to leave their country of origin, hoping to maximise their chance of success.

Migration agencies are often reluctant to categorise travellers such as tourists, visitors, and overseas students as migrants; however, we feel this trend is steadily changing, since it is quite obvious that elements from certain backgrounds among those travellers would not always return to their country of origin on reaching the end of their initial period of residence. Consequently, if they are productive for society, it is fair for us to perceive them as positive migrants and include them in that category.

The Migration Perception Index recognises that the contribution made by migrant societies across the world is a significant proportion of the major economies. In the interests of fair treatment, we firmly believe that controlled immigration is the best form of positive immigration, because the risk of exploitation of both migrants and their hosts is much lower. For example, in the late 1940s positive immigration was used in the UK and it attracted thousands of Indians, Pakistanis and people from the Caribbean to live and work there. As skilled workers they filled positions in occupations such as nursing, transport and light industry. Subsequently many became business owners. In the 1970s, positive immigration inspired thousands of West African youths to move to Spain and Greece, where they became farmers and fishermen. Many centuries earlier, the same pull factor meant that many Europeans migrated to North America, Australia, the Pacific, the Indian sub-continent and Africa. In our perception index, we consider people such as this as positive migrants, in the sense that both migrants and the host country gained mutual benefit with minimal exploitation.

b) Negative immigration

Negative immigration is any form of migration which compels somebody to leave their country of origin, i.e. they are facing circumstances without which they wouldn't otherwise leave. Lack of employment opportunities and conflict are the usual causes of such mass immigration, and it is sometimes referred to it as the 'push' factor. Embarking on such a journey may be hard and long. Occasionally there are success stories claimed by those who have been through it, but disappointment, life-threatening risk and economic uncertainty is very common, and the migrants may become a burden on the people of the country to which they migrate.

This subject is quite delicate, complex and technical. Some people hold the view that it is impossible to truly define who is a negative migrant, because every single migrant considers themselves to be a positive migrant. Migrants are generally perceived to be refugees or economic migrants if they are fleeing from prostitution, family conflict, civil war, famine, poverty, and disease, kidnapping or human traffickers.

For example, in 2015 approximately one million Syrians emigrated from the Middle East to Germany. Most were fleeing war and prostitution. However, some of them were not considered to be genuine refugees: instead they were perceived to be economic migrants who hoped for a better future in Europe. In contrast, from their own perspective, they thought themselves to be positive migrants who are willing to participate and contribute to the economy of Germany.

According to reliable sources, it is estimated that, from 2014 to 2017, roughly eight hundred thousand people moved to mainland Europe from different parts of Africa and Asia claiming to be genuine asylum seekers. In reality, as with the Syrians, people were more likely to see them as economic migrants.

As a result, we included both of these examples in our negative immigration perception index in the sense that they were all pushed by a negative factor, and risked becoming a huge burden on their host country. We can see that if other choices were available to them, perhaps they wouldn't have made the decision to migrate.

Another factor which is attributed to negative immigration is the metaphor of brain drain. For instance, foreign governments frequently give scholarships to the brightest and smartest students in third world countries. They give incentives to selected individuals working abroad in the public sector, usually to people who are highly intelligent and truly dedicated in serving their country. Those who earn such scholarships would migrate from A to B, pursuing their goals, and often they are while studying overseas, members of their family will join them. Hence the majority of them would subsequently remain overseas and pursue personal glory instead of returning home to invest their knowledge in the interests of national development. Thus the intellectual void in third world countries is far greater than you might have previously imagined, due to negative immigration.

A similar trend of intellectual exploitation exists with scholarships from religious institutions in the Middle East offered to Africans and South Asians is steadily influencing societal norms, particularly in the areas of cultural simulation and radicalisation. Without doubt, this causes negative immigration in third world countries. Putting this in context, when some of these people return home from studying overseas, many of them have become fanatics or extremists. Such individuals have little or no regard to common values and confrontation is likely. Patience, humility and tolerance in accommodating other people's views are usually absent in these people. Hence, the Migration Perception Index perceives such attributes as the product of negative immigration.

c) The status-driven factor

This factor is a relatively new one in some countries. Despite that, it is the 3rd major factor causing mass immigration from Africa to the West. In modern society, having the ability to freely move between different European countries is undoubtedly a profound privilege to many, and people living in the third world countries are no exception. As a result, the traditional norms such as family connections, social status, the class system and family values are all quite irrelevant when compared to the influence of Western migration. Migration to the West is truly the new vehicle which drives social status. Thus, fear of the culture of snobbery in society has pushed anxiety through the roof, particularly among young people. Aside from emulating certain international football players, the new ideal for many youths in Africa is migration to Europe.

You might wonder why this is the case. There are a number of reasons:

1. People perceived to be role models for youths in Africa are either European or American.

2. Celebrities from Europe or those from European heritage are the people who are the most admired amongst the youth.

3. Most of the jobs available to youths are presently being occupied by those who studied overseas.

Due to this underlying monopoly, their self-worth is precisely measured against those living in the West. Hence, youth shows little interest in education and has no regard for tertiary and vocational education, consequently, dropping out of school and taking the 'back way' to Europe is the norm.

There is clear evidence that access to harmful materials online and exploitation by human traffickers operating underground, as well as the false impression projected by social media of migrants living in the West are all contributing factors to negative immigration. The Migration Perception Index firmly holds the view that the influence of these three elements drives a process of brainwashing, and the so-called 'European dream' is the factor which intoxicates people's imagination and increases risk. As a result, people will set unrealistic goals and then contemplate on how to achieve them. Amazingly, few resort to fulfilling that dream through illegal means such as drug trafficking and armed robbery.

d) The family factor

This is the most legitimate of the four types of immigration, but that doesn't necessarily imply that it is the most productive form of immigration. Human beings would naturally gravitate towards their families and friends under any circumstances. Perhaps on rare occasions they might face risks from xenophobia and racism but neither of these deters migrants with a genuine desire to sponsor family members and friends in order to join them, and vice versa. Such a process usually involves legal and legitimate means; hence the risk is considerably low. But it has some drawbacks, in the sense that in third world countries the family factor has exacerbated the brain drain and puts pressure on public services in developed countries due to overcrowding.

I will not use any shape or form of prejudice or bias against anyone. We hope that our participation in immigration data collection will be productive and fruitful without invading people's privacy. We will offer our help where it is possible. Personally, I would like to thank you all in advance for your kind understanding and humble cooperation.

My aims and objectives are to discourage negative immigration, and encourage positive immigration. I recognise that governments alone cannot achieve this. It also requires significant intervention from NGOs, charities, and community support groups. They all need to come together as one, in order to tackle the obstacles which are pushing and pulling people to migrate.

We strongly believe that poverty and conflict are no longer the only factors which cause negative immigration. We should also include issues like 'brain drain', an individual's lack of resilience and self-esteem, and the perception that 'the grass is always greener on the other side of the fence'. These, and more, are contributing factors responsible for mass migration in our modern society, and need to be tackled coherently.

My paradigm

*We believe that if communities have access to adequate resources, some of the issues outlined here are quite easy to address. However, others are profoundly technical and complex, and there is no 'silver bullet' solution. Despite the apparent decline in prevalence of 'push' and 'pull' factors, we nonetheless include them in our conversation because we think they are still relevant to the discussion. We collect our data by measuring immigration in four different categories: **positive immigration, negative immigration, the status-driven factor, and the family factor**. When we have sufficient data from the relevant institutions, we will create a demographic index for each country in terms of how many migrants it produces, their intended destination, and how many are likely to be at risk from negative migration. In the interest of accuracy, we aimed to collaborate with government institutions, migration organisations and academic centres.*

2

The AU and EU have a moral obligation to prevent slavery in Libya

People around the world are celebrating the coming of 2018 with a high expectation that the New Year will be more prosperous than the last. I join the international community in hoping this is so. However, we should bear in mind that thousands of African migrants are still languishing in slavery at labour camps and detention centres across Libya. I am pleased to see that certain countries in Africa, like the Gambia, are repatriating their citizens from Libya and persuading other countries to follow their example. However, I hope that conversations about slavery will continue to make headlines around the world, in order to ensure that we put enough pressure on authorities to put an immediate end to slavery, wherever it is happening.

There is a growing suspicion that economic agreements signed between the EU and armed gangs in Libya are encouraging criminals to enslave African migrants who are trying to reach Europe by crossing the Mediterranean Sea through Libya. Therefore desperate youths will be discouraged from taking such a dangerous journey, and Europe will then have fewer illegal immigrants. Even though this theory sounds genuine to some people, I don't want believe such a wild claim is true. I don't think, in the

21st century, the EU would sanction that kind of unimaginable human rights abuse of migrants. However, in ancient times, these methods were occasionally used by powerful states to ensure that law and order was effectively maintained in lawless countries like Libya.

I do understand that whenever a country is confronted by a migrant crisis, there is no easy solution. When I was recently visiting Australia, there was a huge public outcry concerning the status of refugees and economic migrants who are still held in the refugee camp at Manus Island, in Papua New Guinea, under the control of the Australian authorities. With many others, I signed a petition to put pressure on the Australian government to make sure they allow these refugees to settle in mainland Australian. The governments counter argument is that allowing them to settle in the country would mean victory for people traffickers who are making millions of dollars through such a lucrative business. In my opinion such an argument and returning the boats makes more sense than encouraging criminals and gangs to enslave migrants elsewhere.

On the other hand, the behaviour of some economic migrants who are now living in mainland Europe is not helping campaigners like me, who are tirelessly advocating on their behalf. For an example, last week, I was stunned when I saw two videos emerge on Facebook of Gambian migrants based in Germany, ranting in Mandinka and using a Boko Haram type of rhetoric, treating terror in the Gambia if they were deported back to Gambia. According to them, there was a rumour that the

Gambian government had signed an agreement with Germany regarding the deportation of illegal Gambian migrants. I was extremely disappointed by the people who made such threatening videos, and by those who liked it on Facebook.

Discussion concerning economic migration and slavery, especially in Libya, has to be constructive, based on mutual respect, ethics and discipline. But threatening to unleash terror on innocent people will only make the situation for migrants in Europe worse, and those guilty of any wrong doing would have to face the ultimate consequences for their actions. Let's continue our debate with maturity and discipline, not with violence and contempt.

It's always important to remember that we were all created equal. No man is a slave to any other man.

The Gambian government needs to do more to ensure that the human rights of its citizens in Libya and elsewhere are respected

Right now, the international community is making a huge noise with regard to the upheaval of illegal migration which, according to some, is affecting the resources of major economies around the world. However, in my opinion, criminals who continue to enslave African migrants in Libya ought to be the primary concern. In the past few days, I noticed that major news outlets and users of social media are distracting people from this important topic to other less significant political matters (such as the "fire and fury" concerning the psyche of Donald Trump and the recent scuffle between supporters of UDP and APRC in the Gambia).

According to IOM, the lives of thousands of migrants are currently at risk from gangs across Libya. I am begging the international community to continue this discussion and strive to be more vocal to ensure that this immoral practise in Libya and elsewhere is immediately ceased.

In a civilised society, there should never be any correlation between illegal migration and enslaving innocent people against their wills. Illegal migration is a major problem which profoundly requires its own discussions and its own solution. But enslaving human beings against their will is categorically wrong under any circumstances. Regardless of your culture, common sense would dictate that an ambitious youth who is both hopeless and desperate, trying to migrate elsewhere and hoping for a better future, does not deserve to be enslaved!

As I stated in my last article, the moral obligation to tackle and prevent such a heinous crime is not only confined to the EU and AU, but rather a moral obligation on each and every one of us.

Situations such as this often require both short-term and long-term solutions. I would suggest the following four steps:

1. There is a moral obligation on families and friends to discourage their love ones from using the 'back way' through Libya or Morocco which are the main hubs for enslaving African migrants right

now. And they ought to encourage family members who are stranded in these two countries to immediately return home at the first available chance.

2. There is a moral obligation on people like me to make sure that we continue the discussion concerning this matter every day until slavery is stopped.

3. There is a moral obligation on us to participate whenever there are public demonstrations to draw the attention of the international community and put extra pressure on authorities in order for them to do more, like the demonstrations we have witnessed in the streets of London, Paris, New York and in Africa.

4. I understand that the Gambia's government cannot use the migrant crisis in Libya and Europe as a bargaining chip to solicit more aid from the European Union. However, if the Gambia government hasn't made any deal yet concerning the migrant crisis with the EU, as they claimed last week, then they have a moral duty to appeal to EU countries to grant temporary working visas for at least two years to Gambian migrants who went Europe through the 'back way' and are now illegally scattered across Europe, before enforcing any deportation.

While suggesting these short-term solutions, I think it's extremely important for me to also point out and emphasis that the EU, like any continent, has a moral obligation to respect the concerns of its citizens regarding issues surrounding migrants. In addition to that, they have the legal right to remove anyone from their country if they wish, particularly those who they see as illegal immigrants. We have to understand that whatever helps the EU might offer African countries concerning this matter would purely be based on humanitarian grounds. They don't have any legal obligation whatsoever to allow illegal migrants to stay.

As a migrant living in Europe, there is a moral obligation on all of us to recognise that allowing us to remain in mainland Europe is a privilege. It is not an entitlement or a God-given right. As a result, it is our collective responsibility to ensure that we always maintain peace and tranquillity in European society.

Migrants who were lucky enough to make it to Europe after escaping slavery in Libya should come forward and share their experience with the wider world in order to enlighten those who are might be tempted to embark on such a reckless journey. Migrants should also acknowledge the generosity which is always accorded to them by Europeans. They rescue migrants from the peril of the open sea and show them love and kindness, which brings many a step closer to fulfilling a meaningful life in Europe. In my view, showing such appreciation would effectively ridicule the allegations and misconception of those who often claim that the EU is secretly collaborating with Arab gangs in Libya to enslave African migrants in the country.

After all, please remember that, we were all created equal.
No man is a slave to another man.

3

The horror of the Back Way journey to Europe

In March 2017, when I visited central Morocco, the epicentre of the back way to Europe; the purpose of my trip to the country was initially not concerned with investigating the situation of the migrants who use the country as a gateway to Europe. However, since this burning issue is of great interest to me, I decided to pay a courtesy call to two makeshift camps, located in the cities of Fez and Casablanca respectively. I can confirm to you that the condition in which those people live is appalling.

My encounter with a young Senegalese migrant

The first camp which I had visited was a makeshift camp called "The African Villa". This camp is situated near the main train station in Fez. Mr. Jallow, the Senegalese man who welcomed me there, has been stuck in the camp for three years. According to him, since he entered Morocco back in 2015, he has given over $3,500 to human traffickers, but they have not arranged a passage to Europe for him. In that camp alone, there were over five hundred migrants from various countries across Africa. I noticed that the majority of them came from Mali, Guinea Conakry, Senegal and Nigeria.

I asked Mr. Jallow: why would someone risk everything in taking such a journey with huge uncertainty ahead, including the threat of enslavement in a foreign land? He told me:

"My friend, though I have to admit it's really tough in here, it's not a cowardly journey as many people would presume! It's a quest, seeking a better life elsewhere with more opportunity, rather than sitting down at home in Africa wasting my life doing nothing. For me, it is just a window of opportunity to pursue my potential in Europe. In my opinion, whoever dies in such a process surely he or she would achieve martyrdom."

I will share more of my experience in Morocco, and the full conversation I had with Mr. Jallow, in a subsequent book.

This particular camp was the most horrible place I have ever seen. I was horrified at the total lack of basic human needs, e.g. toilets, running water, electricity and medicine for sick migrants. The migrants have no human rights and they live by the so-called law of the jungle. Sadly, their livelihood entirely depends on begging in the street and charity hand-outs from locals. Shockingly, they are not driven to Europe by fear of poverty: it is the fear of a lack of status which leads them to such modern-day slavery. Despite living in such desperate circumstances, none of them wanted to return to Africa until they could fulfil their wild dream of standing on European soil. Often, they receive late night phone calls from their families and friends in Africa who pressurise them and encourage them to carry on, no matter what.

The 'status-driven factor' is the main virus causing mass youth exodus to Europe

Despite the threat of being enslaved in North Africa, a growing number of our youths are still risking their lives migrating to Europe, seeking wealth and glory and hoping for a better future. The dominant theory behind this mass exodus is the old fashioned concept of the push and pull factor, which I discuss at great length in my book Marriage and Society (2014).

However, recently I discovered that there is a third reason why African youth are risking everything to reach European soil. It's what I call "the status-driven factor". From 2017, due to fear of slavery in Libya, Morocco is once again the main hub for desperate migrants seeking to enter Europe illegally.

Around 2012, most people, including me, believed that African youths using the back way to reach Europe did so because of oppression by repressive regimes, ethnic conflict, poverty, famine and lack of employment opportunities. These underlying issues are no longer the cause. They go to Europe because of status anxiety, fuelled by the ridiculous fantasy of getting rich quickly, with no need to have a quality education. The 'status-driven' factor is the new elephant in the room.

An EU official who visited the Gambia recently was at Banjul international Airport receiving some migrants who didn't reach Europe and were persuaded to return home through the Gambian government's repatriation program. He said "It appeared to me as if [the migrants] are feeling shame and are scared to face their families and loved ones, who think such a homecoming is degrading and humiliating." Most people considered these youths a failure for our society. I could not agree more with him, but such humiliation for migrants is not due to a fear of poverty or facing prostitution but it was rather a fear of lack of status.

Apparently, it costs at least $3,000 to migrate from the Gambia to Europe. The human traffickers are making a fortune from this lucrative business, often as much as $5,000 per person (though these figures are just based on a rough estimate depending on the individual's experience). The usual method to raise this money is by selling a plot of land in the urban area, or selling livestock in the rural area or occasionally, using cash sent by a family member who already lives in Europe.

Such a fortune, by Gambian standards, is enough to earn someone a decent degree, by funding their education from nursery school all the way to university. Such a sum would also support a small business, and would financially sustain a medium size family for many years. But these methods are no longer attractive to African youth when they see the fake news, on Facebook and elsewhere, of migrants "living the European dream" and showing off their mythical "new found wealth."

Just recently, somebody told me that a few years ago he tried to look for a wife from his own social class but whenever he approached a family for marriage, it ended in failure. However, two years later he risked his life using the back way to Europe, and when he reached Italy, the following week he was immediately offered two girls for marriage from the very people who previously refused his marriage proposal.

The EU ought to realise that, though they have a moral and legal obligation to deport these people, by forcefully removing them from Europe and sending them back home to Africa, they are effectively sending them to destitution and disfranchisement. I cannot compare such a social consequence with anything in Europe, because there is no equivalent there.

There is no room for slavery in our modern societies. I have to admit that whenever I am dealing with subjects such as this, if I fail to echo Hon. Louis Farrakhan or Mr. Malcolm X surely I won't be able to make any relevant points at all. However, even though I am extremely heartbroken by the abhorrent slavery in Libya, I will try not to be compulsive in my language, rather for now I will use diplomatic vocabulary. Like my comrades, I am equally horrified by the shocking pictures emerging from Libya that are circulating on social media concerning forceful slavery of African migrants in labour camps across the country. The evil behind such barbaric acts by North African Arabs does not surprise me because the culture of impunity is supreme in such puritanical societies.

I struggled for a while but I cannot find any better words than this: what puzzles me the most is the culture of silence by religious scholars in North Africa and the Middle East who often silently endorse immoral attitudes toward black people and minorities in the region. It is really shameful and disgraceful. In addition to this, in the pages of many books authored by scholars of Arabia and their intellectual commentators you will find distorted versions of religious texts written to justify such puritanical concepts which are the fruits of slavery and social segregation, and are still profoundly deep rooted in the wider culture of Arab world.

Relatively recently, the OIC, Arab league, EU, AU, and other major international human rights organisations including the Gambia, were robust in their condemnation of a suspected Houthi insurgent missile attack from Yemen against the capital city of Saudi Arabia, Riyadh. Apart from the Gambia, I believe the EU, AU, OIC, Arab league, and other international organisation were slow to acknowledge the serious abuses that have taken place in Libya since the overthrow of Gaddafi.

According to Anti-Slavery International, which is the oldest human rights organisation in the world, more than 46 million people are still kept as slaves in one shape or form. Sadly, the majority of those caught up in these modern-day conditions are either African or people of a dark complexion. I ought to ask the following question, "Less than one hundred years since the evil of the holocaust ,robust international intervention has effectively prevented another holocaust from happening to the Jewish people. But shockingly for more than two hundred years, since the horrors of trans-Atlantic slavery why are similar preventative measures still failing to protect black people from slavery, particularly in Arab countries?"

Of course, I know there are no easy solutions to tackling cultures of discrimination and segregation which are the main causes of slavery, but in my opinion, robust international intervention would effectively reduce the suffering and inhumane treatment of people perceived to be inferior and minorities who are usually the victims of slavery.

I will suggest the following to African governments: you ought to protect your citizens from discrimination and segregation at any cost and empower them to realise their potential in their native countries.

And for now, my message for Africa's youth: understand that you are not inferior to anyone, and you are not a slave to anyone except God. Rise up to the challenges and be the Moses of your time to free your fellow brothers and sisters from slavery across the world. Use all the peaceful means necessary. Enough is enough! It is the time to emulate the actions of our prophet Muhammed, peace be upon him. He and his companions emancipated more than 39,370 slaves during their lifetime in Arabia. Please understand that, all men are created equal. You are not inferior to anyone and you are not slaves to anybody.

The government cannot do it alone

In the past few weeks speculation in the town has increased over the Gambian government seeking youth employment opportunities in the kingdom of Saudi Arabia. I am not an economic expert but I struggle with the idea that Saudi Arabia could soon become the new Silicon Valley for Gambian migrants looking for greener pastures. Due to conflicting stories on social media, it's not yet clear who is behind such a bold initiative. Whoever it is, I can safely assume that 99% of jobs which are likely to be available to Gambians in Saudi Arabia will be manual labour and domestic work.

There are rules and regulations in place for migrant workers in the Gulf States, but due to culture of impunity, implementing them is harder than you can imagine. I am also not sure if the Gambian government actually has adequate resources on the ground to deal with influx of migrants in case of human rights abuse, which is almost inevitable. I am convinced that this speculation is not fake news. It sounds more sophisticated and accurate. So far the position of the Gambian government concerning this matter is slightly ambiguous. Most people are of the view that there are strings attached to the millions of dollars which are moving into the Smiling Coast of Africa since the dawn of the new administration.

But let's be honest, the spectacular generosity of Saudi Arabia in the build up to next year's OIC Islamic summit, which is expected to take place in the Gambia, is entirely welcomed by many, including me! But I will insist that we do not do anything which will mortgage the future of our exuberant youth. People are still extremely sceptical, despite the Ministry of Tourism dismissing the report that the government is about to encourage its citizens to seek jobs in Saudi Arabia. According to them, such a claim is fiction. I hope that is the case! Nonetheless, it's not uncommon for a developing country to reward the generosity of a developed country by providing cheap labour, even if in reality they know it may be a risk.

What we ought to understand is that, despite the noble teachings of the holy Quran, which encourages people to be humble and fight against all form of bigotry, due to adherence to a deep-rooted mediaeval culture, the status of African immigrants in the Middle East and the Gulf States is virtually equal to the status of 17 century Arabian slaves. Occasionally, it may appear as if there is a willingness among the ruling class to tackle such dogma but usually they just spout political rhetoric. My fellow citizens, let me repeat this: implementing rules and regulations to control bigotry is impossible in the Middle East. With the looming mistrust between the ruling elites and the mighty sectarian hegemony which is prevalent in the society, human rights are often preserved only for nobles belonging to the same biological family tree. Hence the majority of employers would deny people their human rights. A virtuous attitude is totally alien to them.

I am a strong proponent of President Barrow, who prioritises reducing youth unemployment in the country and desires to lift people from abject poverty, but I cannot ignore the evidence of brutality against migrant workers in the North Africa and the Middle East which circulates on the media every single day. Dozens of Gambians are already victims of such brutality. Taking all this in to account, if the government continues to ignore the outcry of the people and allows unscrupulous individual s to export Gambian citizens to the Middle East as domestic workers, it is not the action of a wise leadership. It's a time to have conversation in the pursuit of wisdom, in order to enlighten those of our people who think the grass is greener elsewhere.

Does the Gambian government have the power to stop mass deportation?

Nowadays the most important question we can ask is: does the Gambian government actually have the power to stop mass deportation of Gambians from the West? There are many different opinions, but this is my take.

According to international rules and norms, each sovereign state (including The Gambia) is at absolute liberty to distinguish genuine migrants from those thought to be illegal. Consequently, even the mighty USA holds NO power to stop a determined country (let's say Germany, for example, this is not just about African countries) from deporting US citizens as long as the process is legal.

My fellow Gambians, the brutal fact is that the opportunities of a few decades ago, which attracted thousands of Africans to migrate elsewhere in the pursuit of a better life, particularly to greener pastures in Europe, are no longer available today. As result, the EU and the rest of the West are effectively closing their gates in order to curb mass immigration, regardless of the gender or race of the immigrants.

Anti-immigration sentiment triggered Brexit and decisively got Donald Trump elected President of the United States of America. Such a sentiment propels the agenda of the extreme right-wing popular conservatism movement across Europe. Taking all this in to account, in my opinion, mass deportation from the West is not only inevitable, but it would even be necessary, in order to prevent a resurgence of kind of the concentration camps we saw in World War 2.

Most people are of the view that the austerity measures which were put in place back in 2010 were absolutely not necessary. It was a political choice which was designed to discourage people from welfare dependency: they went ahead with it and it economically battered families and ruined the life of millions of lower income earners. Almost nine years later, people are still living with the consequences.

4

Mass deportation to Africa is similar to austerity in Europe

If there are politicians who can inflict such devastating pain on their own citizens just to prove a point, how on earth can we stop them sending immigrants to poverty and destitution?

Since independence, the culture of excessive dependency on foreign aid (with many strings attached) has significantly reduced our ability to appropriately tackle a crisis of mass deportation. The only thing we seem to offer is daily prayers wishing good luck to migrants. We seriously lack the stomach to challenge our developing partners on issues of economic growth and human improvement, let alone migrant welfare. I know the room for diplomatic manoeuvres is often quite small because our limited resources mean we have no bargaining chips, but even so…

African youths lack a genuine desire to pursue a prosperous future in the motherland, so they seek their fortune elsewhere. Blaming the government is not the answer. It's time to start a constructive debate about mass immigration, to Europe, the rest of the West and in our own back yard. The biggest headache for the middle class in the Gambia right now is rural-urban migration, which is putting pressure on limited resources in public services such as hospitals and schools, and increasing the cost of living (let's be honest, the majority of Europeans are suffering from similar challenges).

We ought to proudly open our arms and welcome our dear brothers and sisters who are being deported from the West, and share with them whatever we have, without prejudice against them or hindrance against Europeans. Arguments and public disorder are not beneficial, but unity in finding a peaceful solution and desire to nurture our social cohesion will make a huge difference. Though genuine news and fake news have equal status in their appearance on social media, spreading unfounded stories and inciting violence on Facebook and WhatsApp is not the act of a responsible citizen! People who ignite fireworks on social media cannot expect to boost their legal status in Europe or enhance their chances of claiming political asylum.

Is there any solution?

You are may be wondering, what is the solution to confront mass emigration? Here is my response; I would say that, virtually there is no single solution to it except constructive debates concerning its drawbacks. Nonetheless, the power of "HOW" might be more effective to reduce illegal immigration, instead of asking "WHY". Often when I discuss this subject I realise one thing in particular which intrigues me for a while is that, whenever people have a conversation about mass migration often public opinion would gather a storm on WHY people emigrate from one place to another, rather than have a discussion on HOW to create a conducive environment in order to prevent it from happening in the first place.

For instance, in terms of putting preventive measures in place, the dominant suggestions that people would frequently make are a) job creation, b) youth empowerment, and c) building strong institutions.

But the counter arguments are:

a) Job creation would allow someone to accumulate enough wealth from point A and then immigrate to point B hoping for a better wage incentive.

b) Youth empowerment in terms of providing scholarship and entertainment equipment, and promoting sport means the country risks squandering the most productive members of its society by exporting its most talented citizens to attend overseas events. Often, these are individuals who have a tendency to risk overstaying their visas and then claim political asylum in order to pursue their Western dreams.

c) Institutions built by corrupt individuals would perhaps mean abetting public officials to further embezzle public funds by looting State resources from developing countries in the favour of investing it in developed countries.

Whenever we are confronted with socio-economic difficulties often we ask ourselves WHY such and such happened? And in the absence of cohesive response in order to tackles such dilemma it would usually lead us to anger and frustration. Rather, we ought to ask ourselves HOW to confront such and such, which will usually usher us to have a constructive debate with positive thinking which comes hand in hand with a creative solution. For example, instead of worrying about WHY I failed to have a job for a year, instead focus on HOW to get a job within a year. Again, instead of bothering about WHY I am still single, focus on HOW to find a lifelong partner for myself as soon as possible! Hence, let's have a constructive debate of HOW to reduce mass immigration.

We believe the following three will be useful:

1. Introducing the subject of immigration in the national curriculum.

2. Help people to improve their self-esteem.

3. Diversification of the public concept of ideals of beauty and success.

5

In relation to how colonisation and immigration shapes modern Africa, here is an essay which I published in May 2020.

A pending revolution in Africa

Introduction

The history of Africa is a two-sided coin. On one side you have written accounts and on the other sits the oral version. However, the written accounts are more appealing to academics and researchers than the oral version, because the written accounts usually echo the theories of pseudoscience by medieval Muslim and Christian theologians, who often rely on biased sources, and have depicted the people of the continent as stupid and superstitious. Such a negative perception is still widely accepted by many throughout the globe, and has led to some of the appalling human rights abuse which took place in the continent over the past five hundred years: the transatlantic slave trade, for example.

Due to tribal conflict over power and resources, the oral history of Africa is shot through with fiction and misconception. The proponents of this were the praise singers who seek favour through tribal loyalty to, and the patronage of, the ruling elites, and the oriental Islamic and Christian scholars who were using assimilation through conversion. As a result and in relation to this subject, it is harder to gather authentic information from independent sources with 100% accuracy; because every single opinion has been profoundly influenced by one thing or the other.

You may recall that in the late sixteenth century, most people in Africa reconstructed their family ancestral tree by adopting Middle Eastern and Western ancestral descent, and the true account of the history of Africa since antiquity might have been lost in that process. However, with the use of modern technology, if you test the ancestral DNA of people on the continent, you will discover that actually 99% of those so-called Arabs and Whites are in fact bona fide Africans belonging to a lineage which dates back thousands of generations.

In this essay my discussion will centre mainly on the issues in West Africa. The figures that I give are based on the rough calculations that I have obtained from various internet sources.

I will discuss this in two parts. Let me begin by stating what happened between 1860 and 1910. This period is the post-transatlantic slave trade period, and is commonly known as the Scramble for Africa.

What happened between 1860 and 1910?

The political atmosphere

While the mighty Western aristocrats battled to control the land and resources, the indigenous rulers and elites were busy competing for favours from the colonial masters, not out of love and compassion or sincerity, but rather due to fear and desperation. They were willing to pay homage to the feudalist state by any means necessary. Eventually, the colonial masters introduced an arbitrary tax system as a form of protection fee to ensure that people felt safe and secure from the rival tribes, and the master's own Western opponents. The countries in Africa became known as protectorates of Western countries, whilst giving up their labour, and treasures such as gold, silver and diamonds.

The religious situation

Before the creation of modern states with distinct borders as we know them today, the continent was divided between city states and each state was headed by a local tribal chief with semi-autonomy in his or her kingdom, in charge of tax collection and forced labour. Eventually, these city states became further divided along tribal and sectarian lines (where the infamous 'divide and rule' got its name from), and colonial hegemony was then scattered across the continent.

Christianity existed in the continent for many centuries before the birth of Islam, the dominant religion at this time was Sufi Islam but the prevalence of new Christian missionaries in the region maintained a strong Christian presence. The indigenous religions slowly vanished. A power struggle over nobility between different Muslim sects was at its peak. It was exacerbated by a certain Sufi doctrine regarding the concept of sainthood centuries before the advent of the transatlantic slave trade. Divisions such as this abetted and consolidated the position of Arab slave traders from North Africa.

The education system

In Sub-Saharan Africa at this time, Islamic education and agriculture were central to day to day living because people were entirely dependent on the land and theology. Most people were well-versed in Arabic language and poetry, particularly those written about the life of the noble prophet Muhammad. Families would proudly send children as young as seven to learning centres as far away as Timbuktu in Northern Mali, and Fez in Morocco. The harder they strove to obtain knowledge, the more respect they earned in society. Those from the noble backgrounds would frequently send their children far and wide to seek knowledge. The more they did, the more superior they felt. Consequently, to spend many years of absence seeking knowledge would earn the title of Arafang (graduate), a wife, and status in the family.

At the same time, Western-style education by missionaries was active in Christian monasteries, however the learning was mainly confined to bible studies and Christian theology. It was not as widespread as Islamic education at that stage, but nonetheless local chiefs would often send their children to learn Western languages in order to ease communication barriers. The education was later expanded to include administration and translation, taught to the servants working for colonial administrators such as record keepers, clerks and tax collectors.

The family and the economy

In the absence of modern science, the pre-Islamic history of Africa is quite ambiguous. This is largely due to the influence of the northern culture in the society. Furthermore if we could thoroughly examine the accounts of the thirteenth century Moroccan scholar Ibn Battuta, you would imagine that the manner in which he described Africa and its people in terms of family values and thriving economy, which was not disrupted until the late fifteenth century after the commencement of the transatlantic slave trade.

Although later 75% of the economy was controlled by slave traders and their allies, nonetheless for many centuries the sense of family values and family structure was not entirely disrupted or damaged as some scholars would suggest. It's dubious for people to continue to claim that their family tree goes back to early Muslims from North Africa and later Christians from the West as if there was no family orientation in the continent before its contact with outsiders. To be fair the concept of family reconstruction is common throughout the world, however most people would not take it literally but rather as praise.

But despite that, you may feel good when people praise your family lineage but the drawback of such praise is more severe than you can imagine, because it plays a significant role in shaping the concept of beauty. As a result in Africa some people use skin bleaching and wear hair extensions in order to look like a white person. Additionally, in the Mediterranean, Asia Minor and Iran, people would have cosmetic surgery on their noses just to look like westerners. In Europe, breast augmentation and cosmetic surgery is widespread. For many, it had consequences for their health.

What happened between 1910 and 1960?

The political atmosphere

In this period, 99% of the continent was firmly under colonial rule with an iron fist. Political power was entirely vested in the colonial master. No matter the size, each country was divided into several administrative regions, not according to its pre-colonial structure but into Western-style administrative systems which were more flexible and politically efficient to control. In every region, regional governors or administrative commissioners were at the helm of power.

Less than 10% of the indigenous people were given the task to maintain the law and order in their own locality. Handfuls of small villages combined together under one chieftain, who later became known as the district chief. As you can imagine, managing different tribes with diverse cultures and multiple languages was never going to be easy. Brutality against the local people by the tribal chiefs and their henchmen, acting on behalf of the colonial administration was very disheartening. Such inhumane treatment was widespread throughout the continent.

The religious situation

At this stage, 80% of the population in the continent were either Muslims or Christians. Even though the administrative officers were mostly white Christians from Europe, since the primary objective of colonial masters was to effectively control economy and trade, they made little effort to control religion or to impose their faith on locals. However, the Christian evangelical Anglican social reformers, whose teachings galvanised people like Hon. William Wilberforce some decades earlier, were converting hundreds of thousands of people into Christianity in the towns and cities. Hence Christianity in Africa is still more prevalent in the cities and towns, than in the villages and rural areas.

On the other hand Muslims enjoyed greater autonomy in how they worshipped, and their agriculture. However, the power struggle of fame and popularity between the followers of different Sufi orders eventually engulfed society. The dispute among them was fuelled by the students of mystic scholars belonging to different Tariqas, particularly on the subject of sainthood (who were the saints and how could a person become one?) Such division among Sufi scholars in Africa caused further disunity in the continent, and it gave more ammunition to the colonial masters to oppress people even further.

In order to increase division, the colonial masters would often give favour and sanctuary to those belonging to noble families. In addition to that, they gave the impression that the African nobles were socially equal to contemporary whites and Arab nobles, but only if they could prove their noble family lineage. Consequently, to do that, people began to draft manuscripts known as silsila which they would use as a vessel to carry their family tree back to Adam and Eve. Such a sophisticated dividing technique was imperative for the colonial masters to solicit loyalty among the Sufi community.

Brilliant strategies such as this have continued to shape opinions and often you hear people praising their ancestors or giving credit to their grandfathers or great-grandfathers for the spiritual miracle which they have supposedly performed while helping the colonial masters to win certain wars under difficult circumstances.

However, others like Imam Samori Toure, Sheik Ahmed Taal and Serigne Touba were entirely critical of colonial rule. As a result, Samori Toure, Sheik Taal and many others were slain. Serigne Touba was imprisoned for many years. Eventually he was released but he never enjoyed the same amount of freedom. Insurgents scattered in small groups across the continent called for a holy war against colonial rule, but to no avail. Militia groups like the one headed by Foday Kaba Dumboya massacred thousands of innocent Muslims in the pretext of this so-called holy war.

The education system

For many centuries Islamic education was the dominant form of education in Africa. Theology dominated 70% of all learning, and the rest was poetry and the learning of Sufi mystic knowledge. This included medicine, dream translation, how to make amulets and more. Usually to obtain such scientific training would cost people a fortune. Despite that there was no substitute for it, hence in pursuit of social status, people would travel far and wide to seek such knowledge. The legal system was a common law presided over by the government, but theology was central to family matters and social norms, and was hugely influential in business also, thus it has been given particular emphasis.

Until then the Christian missionary schools were mainly learning centres for bible studies. As previously mentioned, around this period, the offspring of the ruling elites were steadily going to school to learn administration and Western languages. Yet in order for outsiders to access such a privilege, first they had to convert to Christianity, or change their name to a Christian name, otherwise they risked losing the opportunity of going to school. Almost instantly the floodgates for Western education opened not, for the few but for many. It is precisely why in the countries where Christianity is the dominant religion, Western education is more advanced than Arab and indigenous education. Arguably this is the period of enlightenment in Africa. Eventually people would travel overseas to learn more about philosophy, politics, medicine, and the economy. Western education laid the foundation for people to seek independence and self-determination, both in Africa and elsewhere.

The family and the economy

Although the majority of people were poor and destitute, the sense of family values and unity was extremely important for social cohesion. Due to colonial oppression and other social factors, life expectancy was low, therefore, in order to sustain population growth, early marriage was crucial. Infectious diseases like malaria and TB chiefly contributed to pandemic child mortality and human extinction. Poor diet was a major hindrance for healthy population growth. For example, out of every ten children, probably only four would live to celebrate their fortieth birthday.

Traditional practises such as male and female genital mutilation, and initiation, were prevalent at all levels. These were mainly conducted in secret ceremonies. Villagers would select a particular location in the bush where they would gather the youth to learn about certain aspects of culture concerning African traditions, social norms and codified rules. They would stay in the bush for at least a month or so. During that period, adults would transmit their skills orally to their children to ensure that outsiders could not easily acquire this knowledge.

90% of population entirely depended on agriculture, either through farming, livestock or fishing. Almost every household owned some sort of livestock. Everybody would equally participate in farming: man, woman, or child. Family disputes were usually settled amicably without resorting to help from the authorities. The biggest disadvantage for society was social stratification which was pretty strict at the time. It created huge challenges for social mobility. Inter-marriage between different tribes was not encouraged and people from a lower class wouldn't marry those in an upper class. Nonetheless maintaining a good reputation in the family and observing respect for elders with honour was the goal for everyone. Common forms of entertainment were African music and wrestling.

Unintended revolution

I will discuss this in four parts: from 1960 to 1985, from 1985 to 2010, from 2010 to 2035 and finally from 2035 to 2060.

The period of hustle - what happened between 1960 and 1985?

The political atmosphere

In this period, almost 95% of countries in Africa attained independence and self-determination. But just a few decades earlier Africans fought alongside Europeans in the first and second world wars with victory at the expense of more than 80 million lives. Fighting alongside Europeans who were then struggling to gain freedom from the Nazis and Fascism awakened a giant within the African psyche: "If we could fight to secure freedom and liberty for others, then what about our own freedom and independence?" Such resilience was the tree which bore the fruit for seeking independence. It sparked an unintended revolution into action.

Although the writing was already on the wall for a motion towards independence, would it have occurred had it not been for the consequences of war? I doubt it would, and I will elaborate more on that in the final segment. The opinions and philosophies of black nationalists like Marcus Garvey and Martin Luther King Jr, and black radicals like Malcolm X and W.E.B. Du Bois, were not widely mobilizing people at the time due to these stumbling blocks.

Firstly, information was tightly controlled by a handful of authorities. Secondly, books and newspapers were heavily censored, and thirdly, due to social taboo and political immaturity, except in the field of entertainment, the opinion of the children of slaves in the Caribbean and America didn't carry much weight in continental Africa, and that remained the case for many years. Miraculously somehow they did galvanise independence fighters like Kwame Nkrumah, Sekou Toure, Patrice Lumumba and Julius Nyerere. The sacrifice that these noble men made for Africa has laid a strong foundation for liberation movements in the continent. But it was just sheer luck to have the independence. Before independence our situation wasn't different from that of people in the Pacific Ocean. We could have still been living under a colonial system like New Caledonia and Tahiti, because they lacked technology and the means to defend themselves.

The religious situation

Islam and Christianity continued to denominate all forms of worship in the continent, yet slowly the Rastafarian movement which developed in Jamaica in the early 1930s, influenced by the philosophy and opinion of Marcus Garvey, was gaining popularity in Africa. Rastafarians don't have a central creed like Islam and Christianity, but they encourage their followers to respect Mother Nature and smoke cannabis as well as resistance against colonial rule. They forged a common identity around reggae music, dreadlocks and wearing the flag mixed with different colours which symbolises Garvey's vision for black unity. The movement hasn't constituted a special form of worship, however Jesus of Nazareth and the Emperor of Ethiopia, Haile Selassie, are revered figures. The Jamaican reggae star Bob Marley and Alpha Blondy in the Ivory Coast, for example, are big icons for the movement.

Until this time, not many Muslims in Africa could afford to travel to Mecca as pilgrims due to economic hardship. However, with the advent of convenient transportation systems by air, land and sea, the number of pilgrims to Saudi Arabia from Africa has significantly increased from hundreds per annum to hundreds of thousands every year. Another factor which has contributed to this increase was youth emigration to Europe from the early 1960s which brought about economic advantage for many. The period has also witness the emergence of visitation to Sufi shrines and tombs of venerated saints, commonly known as Ziyarat, in addition to Mawlid Nabi, the annual celebration of the Prophet Muhammad's birthday. Simultaneously Christian evangelists were also getting a foothold in central and Southern Africa with a large following.

The education system

For the first time in history. foreign governments were competing to provide scholarships for African students so that they could pursue a higher education overseas. The Commonwealth scholarship was introduced for people in the Commonwealth countries, with similar packages were available for those in the French and Portuguese speaking countries as well. Gradually the traditional Christian missionary schools were converted to government-controlled state schools. Compulsory requirement to be a Christian for school entry was finally abolished. Thus, Western education was finally accessible for all. Rich parents who could afford it would send their children to study overseas.

Mali, Morocco and Mauritania, which used to be the major learning centres for Muslim students for centuries were no longer as effective as Egypt, Libya, Sudan and Saudi Arabia. And as a result in the 1960s, Muslim students in Africa began to travel in their thousands to seek knowledge in Egypt and Sudan. In the 70s, thanks to billions of dollars of oil revenue, Libya and Saudi Arabia introduced a Western-style scholarship system for students in Africa.

It weakened the local Islamic Majlis education in Africa and chiefly contributed to the sharp decline of Sufism in the continent. Tertiary education hadn't gathered momentum at the time, but local people were actively involved in carpentry, building, mechanical work, cloth fabrication. Adults were encouraged to participate in night classes in order to enhance their skills in farming and horticulture. Then eventually, Arabic schools were established alongside the Western schools, first by those who studied in Libya and Egypt, and later by students from Saudi Arabia and elsewhere.

The family and the economy

From the early 60s to the mid 80s, the number of women graduating from high school dramatically increased from 10 to 40%, hence women were competing with men in the labour market and as result they became more financial independent. Polygamy, which used to be appealing to many was then no longer attractive (in Africa at least 90% of the population were born into polygamous families). Furthermore, levirate marriage, sororate marriage and early child marriage were also no longer encouraged. Young women were migrating from villages and towns into cities, looking for similar opportunities to men. In hindsight, the rapid social change of the frequent rural to urban migration may have greatly contributed to the emergence of prostitution in the 80s in major towns and cities, in addition to drug and alcohol abuse. Petty crime and the antisocial behaviour of the youth rapidly increased and STDs and HIV/AIDS plagued the continent.

To migrate from one place to the other looking for greener pastures was as rampant in Africa as in other continents. People travel between different countries looking for opportunities. For the first time since the early 1960s, Africans freely travelled in large numbers to Europe and America, not as slaves, but as free men and women and not only for study, but to hustle and make money. Cheap labour in Europe which commenced after the Second World War may have been the main factor here.

The first journeys were from Africa to Greece and Spain and then into Scandinavia. The stories of those early travellers later become synonymous with "sea men". They gave birth to so many fairy tales, such as white women's infatuation for black men. The infamous romantic affairs between African men and Scandinavian women in the 60s and 80s was one example. As a result, tourism from Germany and Scandinavia quickly developed between Europe and Africa. It later complemented the economy. Hotels were built, nightclubs were created and restaurants were opened.

The second wave of migrants to Europe were African healers mainly from Mali, Guinea Conakry, Senegal, Mauritania and Morocco, who moved to France. As I said earlier, the advent of Arab and Western education caused the decline of Sufi Islamic education in Africa. Such a sudden power shift shocked the foundation of Sufism to its core. Farming and handouts from students were no longer sufficient for survival, so the migrants felt that the grass was greener on the other side of the fence. They went to France because the majority of them came from French-speaking countries. Other countries in Africa followed them.

95% of African healers (marabouts) who arrived in Europe settled in France for almost 30 years before they gradually scattered throughout the continent. Note: though divination, astrology, clairvoyant, mediums and fortune tellers are widespread in Africa, you cannot conflate them with marabout. A marabout is a Sufi teacher who gives blessings to people through intense prayers and guides them to righteousness. This remains the dominant form of spiritual healing in Africa and elsewhere.

The period of individual interest - what happened between 1985 to 2010?

The political atmosphere

In this period the remaining 5% of the continent all gained their independence; Namibia, South Africa, Eritrea, and South Sudan. However, due to a weak security structure and inadequate economic system Africa lacked strong institutions hence it remained fragile and poor. Civil war was widespread in the continent. From the 1960s to the 2000s, Africa experienced four types of wars.

1. A war for independence, as happened in Zimbabwe, Kenya, Algeria, Guinea Bissau, Angola, etc. In each country there is an opposition consisting of individuals who once served in the government but for some reason they fell out of favour with the rulers.

2. A civil war between different ethnic groups who were competing to control land and resources as

happened in Congo, Liberia, Sierra Leone, Rwanda, Burundi, etc.

3. Armed separatists fighting for autonomy e.g. the Biafran war in Nigeria, the war between separatists in Casamance and Senegal, the war between South Sudan and mainland Sudan, the war between South Africa and Namibia, the war between Ethiopia and Eritrea, etc.

4. Religious conflicts between modernists and extremists e.g. Boko Haram in Nigeria, Al-Shabaab in Somalia, Al Qaeda in Mali, Isis in Libya, Janjaweed in Sudan, etc. These were proxy wars. It is alleged that often the protagonists received their funding from outside the country.

Another challenge for the post-independence Africa was the military coup d'état. In the continent, except for Mauritius and Botswana, peace in every country has been disrupted in one form or another, often caused by a military take-over of a civilian government. You might say imperial Marxism from the East fought capitalism in the West to control Africa's resources. And yet in this chaotic situation, neo-colonial institutions such as the IMF and the World Bank bullied people to introduce a multi-party system, which divided people even further. In order to ruin the economy further, the two giants then took centre stage by offering foreign aid, which was totally unnecessary. Such a foreign policy has created a culture of dependency in statecraft and it encourages more corruption and financial embezzlement. Above all, they have brainwashed our leaders to take loans which were unnecessary.

The religious situation

At this stage, the adherence to the most strict form of orthodox Islam known as Salafism gained a foothold in the continent. The proponents of this doctrine were the Sunni clerics who had studied in the Middle East and North Africa in the 70s and 80s and had now returned home. First they succeeded to establish Islamic emirates in nine states in Northern Nigeria under Islamic Sharia law. Possibly, the distorted texts that they received from the Middle East and the intolerant version of Islam that they teach in schools, as well as their contempt of modernity, may have contributed to insurgency in Nigeria, Mali, Somalia, Chad, Algeria, Morocco and Burkina Faso.

Before then the Maliki jurisprudence school of thought was the dominant Islamic theology in North and West Africa. The Shafi jurisprudence school of thought was popular in East and Central Africa. Yet by the power of literature, which is disseminated through the airwaves, gradually the puritanical Salafi belief system became the most feared version of Islam in the continent and caused a massive division and confrontation among the Muslim communities.

Through their endowment projects of Saudi Arabia, Kuwait and the Emirates, they have built thousands of mosques and learning centres across Africa. The majority of imams at these mosques, and 98% of teachers at these Islamic schools, were all clerics who have studied in the

Middle East. They encourage their students to dress like their counterparts in the Middle East. Thus men would grow their beads long like Arab men, and women would wear head scarves like Arab women. It has created a massive trade in Arab literature and textiles between the Middle East and Africa. However, it has prohibited social fraternity between men and women, and to socialise with non-Muslims is discouraged.

On the other hand, pilgrimage to Mecca has rapidly increased from 10% in the 60s to 65% in the 90s. Thus now, 6 out of 10 people who meet the criteria to perform the hajji have travelled to Saudi Arabia to complete this religious obligation at least once in their lifetime. The advent of air travel and remittance from overseas has made it more easy and convenient. It also became the custom for politicians to provide free hajji packages to a handful of their individual party supporters. Big businesses in certain countries have also started to sponsor free hajji packages to some of their loyal customers, and Saudi Arabia has provided free hajji packages for its clerics in Africa. Meanwhile, pilgrimages to seek blessings from Sufi tombs and visitation to the shrines of people thought to be saints became part of the social norm. It has steadily increased from the 1980s to date., with no sign yet of a decline. Thanks to remittance from overseas, every year families would spend fortunes to commemorating the demise of their loved ones, usually a leader of a clan belonging to a particular notable family. Many believe that such a practise will bring luck and respect to the family. 75% of villages, towns and cities across Africa organise large gatherings such as this. It is commonly known as the annual ziyarat, or the recitation of the holy Quran for the family. The Salafi puritanical campaign discouraged people from taking part in musical festival pilgrimages, which had been common in villages and towns for centuries.

This was also a period which witnessed the emergence of Christian pastors, who often claimed to be prophets and that they could cure diseases and perform miracles. T.B Joshua from Nigeria and Prophet Shepherd Bushiri from Malawi are two examples. Throughout this period, apart from the Lord Resistance Army in Angola and Uganda, there was no militia group which declared war on behalf of Christianity in Africa, and there was no known report of child abuse at the hands of bishops in the churches, as was claimed elsewhere.

The education system

In this period, education became a priority for many countries. At school, girls were given similar opportunities to boys and that encouraged many parents to send their daughters to school. For the first time in history, private schools were built and they became really popular. However most parents couldn't afford to send their children to private schools: there were lower fees in government-run schools. Because of low salary, a teaching job was a less attractive job for many. The benevolence of charities like Action Aid and Catholic Relief Services immensely contributed to the provision of meals for school children. To wear a school uniform became compulsory, and each school had its own distinct colour. Then tertiary education was introduced. In urban areas, children would travel by state-provided buses to school, and in rural areas they would usually have to walk a few kilometers before reaching school.

After obtaining the common entrance certificate from primary six, most students would immigrate to urban areas in order to pursue higher education. To find a place to lodge in the cities was extremely challenging for most pupils. It put a lot of pressure on extended families and the government to provide sanitation for students from rural areas. It's the primary reason why in the 70s and 80s most children would drop out of school in third world countries due to lack of accommodation in the cities.

The curriculum in Arabic schools was quite similar to standardised Western school curriculums. It included maths, science, grammar, history, geography, literature and theology. In stark contrast to Majlis learning centres, Arabic schools taught 99% theology and Sufi mystic knowledge. This makes Arabic schools more preferable for many. The scholarships which were available in Arabic schools were an extra advantage. However, the labour market for Arabic students was quite saturated, because they could only became imams and teachers. Majlis students had the opportunity to become imams, marabouts, farmers, businessmen, and teachers.

The family and the economy

At this stage, colonialism was entirely ended and each country celebrated the day it obtained independence. Artificial governments were then put in place and 99% of administrative roles were vested in indigenous people. From the outset it appeared as if the governments were in charge of affairs but in reality they weren't. The land and its resources was micromanaged by the Washington Consensus institutions. With their heavy debt, the majority of these governments failed to provide adequate infrastructure for basic services such as health, education, defence and agriculture. Salaries for civil servants were below the poverty line, which gave rise to corruption and nepotism.

An aspect of corruption is more cultural than anything else. For example, a taxi driver would only declare half of what he made to his boss, and a police officer would demand a bribe from that taxi driver. In order for that officer to be promoted, he would share the bribe with his boss, who would also have to bribe someone else at the top in order for him to remain in his position. The person at the top would have to bribe all the way to the head of state. The head of state would then give the same money back to the community in order to buy their loyalty. So in essence corruption is part of society in one form or another.

In order to improve the communication, roads and bridges were built and they became the chief method of travel. Motor vehicles, motorbikes, bicycles and donkey-carts were imported from Europe in large numbers. It was prestigious to own a motor vehicle. Ordinary people living in the city were able to access running water, electricity, telecommunications and television sets. In sport, football gradually replaced wrestling in popularity. Reggae music, rap and R&B become popular among the youth, and traditional music remained attractive for adults. In most countries information was tightly controlled by the government via a handful of radio stations. Some countries didn't have a TV station.

The major contributor to GDP was tax, agriculture, public service and foreign aid. Later down the line, in some countries tourism would contribute 22% of the annual GDP and remittance from overseas was at 25%. Due to rural-urban migration, property prices sky-rocketed. Migrant workers who were returning from Europe would usually settle in the cities and as result the demand for land pushed the price to an all-time high. A high percentage of youths had either already migrated to the West or were about to emigrate, by any means necessary. For the first time in history, earning money and status in the West replaced the importance of family values and good character in Africa.

The period of status – 2010 to 2035

In the remaining sections, my discussion will focus on the prevailing situation in both Africa and Europe, and the future.

The political atmosphere

By this time corruption, armed conflict, disease and illiteracy, which were deep rooted in the continent for decades, now escalated to a new level, and ignited antigovernment sentiment. Political dissidents jumped on the bandwagon and sought refuge in the West. Some were genuine but many are not. Though it is hard to give an accurate figure concerning corruption, in 2013 the AU report about corruption suggested that Africa would lose at least $148 billion per annum through various kinds of corruption (source - allAfrica.com). However, according to a rough estimate from other sources, between 1960 and 2010, Africa lost $800 billion through corruption. Nigeria alone stood at $400 billion.

Armed conflict declined rapidly but each year, millions of people died from infectious diseases, and 35% of the population is still illiterate.

In the West

Ever since they started arriving, first as students and then later as migrant workers, Africans were welcomed by the people in the West. From the 1960s until the late 1990s, there was no great hostility towards migrants, in fact the majority of them were given the chance to easily legalise their immigration status. Amazingly until the early 80s, countries like Britain, Portugal and France would give automatic citizenship to people who came from their former colonies. Except in France, military service was not compulsory, but nonetheless many migrants proudly joined the army to serve their hosts. Despite that, but in every country there were 'no go' areas for migrants.

Third world industry

In post-industrial Europe after the Second World War, the majority of migrant workers who arrived in Europe worked in factories and construction. Some worked as transport workers and hospitality workers in hotels and restaurants. 95% of them earned their living through legitimate means. Due to lower wages they could only afford to live in deprived areas, often in small ghettos. And thanks to their tribal mentality, African people would often create their own separate ghettos, well apart from Caribbeans and other blacks. Such attitudes caused divisions between black people in the West and laid a solid foundation for drug smuggling and gang rivalry.

African Muslims joined other Muslim communities, and a few Christians have also merged into their community, in stark contrast to Asians. Regardless of their rigid caste system back home, Indians from the Indian sub-continent, from Africa and the Pacific united in the West as one community, creating businesses, establishing community centres, and building schools and many places of worship. It vindicated people like me who often argue that the division among blacks communities in the West hasn't got anything to do with our colonial past. Instead it has everything to do with our tribal differences which we have inherited. Asians from all over the world have endured similar mistreatment to Africans in the past, but due to their strong sense of family and unity, what Indians have collectively achieved in the West is unmatched.

Media politics

The rivalry cause by disunity among the black population eventually reached a boiling point. Armed conflict between gangs was then inevitable. To earn a living through legitimate means was no longer desirable for some, and as result they resorted to drug dealing alongside whites and Asians. But for some reason black people were singled out as the source of the problem and they became synonymous with violence and drugs. Then Hollywood and the mainstream news took advantage of the situation. Biased reporting in the news took centre stage (knife crime in London and gang violence in Chicago, for example). Black actors in blockbuster films made in Hollywood portrayed murderers, drug dealers, thieves and bank robbers: always the bad guy. Additionally they have been depicted in children's films and literature as unintelligent.

These blockbuster movies, intended to tarnish the good image of black people, were then distributed across Africa and elsewhere. Ignorant of the agenda behind such films, television stations and cinemas across Africa would play these films repeatedly. Consequently, the children in Africa would emulate what they have seen on the screen. It gave them the impression that in the West you cannot make money quickly without resorting to violence and drug smuggling. Furthermore, rap music which often promotes antisocial behaviour and gang violence was later added to the mix. Taking all this into account, in the 80s and 90s a high percentage of Africans living in Germany, Switzerland, Spain, Italy, UK and the USA. were all taking part in drug smuggling.

The religious situation

Throughout this period moderate Muslims and Christian evangelists continued to dominate the continent. However, the orthodox Salafi were gradually increasing in popularity as well. Meanwhile the Mourides in Senegal, founded by Sheikh Amadou Bamba, were also increasing their followers. The Senegalese historian Cheikh Anta Diop said that "Mouride is the only branch of Islam which has originated in Africa, and some day it will reach every corner of the continent." Africans in the diaspora continued to sponsor their families back home to enable them to perform the hajji in Mecca. And yet in the West they didn't built enough churches and mosques: instead they preferred to worship in the other people's prayer grounds.

Education

In pursuit of the United Nations Millennium Development Goals to ensure that extreme poverty and HIV/AIDS are halted in the world, most countries in Africa have introduced a free basic education system. Countries such as Zimbabwe and Equatorial Guinea would project their literacy rate as between 98 and 99%. The Gambia and Senegal would project theirs to be 86-87%. But overall, education in Africa lacks quality, because the learning system which is based on the curriculum created to complement colonial rule remains the same. People only go to school just to pass exams and then look for a job. Education is not intended for human advancement or capacity building. To make matters worse, the dependency culture which was created by foreign aid and the remittance from overseas children means that people are no longer motivated to learn. The more free money you give them, the more lazy they become.

In the West

In 2015, the former British Prime Minister Sir John Major questioned British educational standards and records on tackling inequality. There are so many conspiracy theories concerning the migrant children. Some make sense but many don't.

There are two dominant theories. One argument is this: teachers would often provoke black kids in the classroom in order to sabotage their education. The other argument is that biased educational psychologists from colonial times have suggested that the black kids have a lower IQ, thus they haven't got the same potential for learning as others. Therefore, it's "okay" for schools to discriminate against them.

They might sound convincing, but let's be honest, none of these arguments puts sugar in my tea. I had many conversations about this with people who have been to school, however since I had never been to school, I may have been oblivious of certain facts. But again, I would draw parallels with Asians. Indians are some of the most intelligent people in the West and I cannot imagine the education system across the West would use bias against the blacks in the favour of whites and Indians. Nevertheless black kids continue to drop out of school;

and most thrive in sport and music more quickly than mainstream education.

Although they may look sincere from the outset, in reality scholarship is the single source of brain drain to the West and the East that Africa experiences. Due to attractive wages in the West, students with scholarships don't return to invest their knowledge in the continent. A minority among them return to work for multinational corporations, such as oil and mining companies. These giants are the major hindrance to economic growth in Africa. Those young men and women are highly intelligent people. The public sector and small business needs them. Additionally, scholarship to the Middle East has significantly accelerated the assimilation process for Salafis in Africa. Had they not been brainwashed in the Middle East many among these intelligent men and women could be revolutionaries who would spearhead the cultural nationalism in Africa which is well overdue.

The family and the economy

The advent of migration to the West from the 60s has slowly ruined the concept of family values in Africa. Nowadays money and status is where all value lies. Parental authority has dwindled to an all-time low. Young people hardly observe respect for adults. Perhaps globalization may have played a role in this but not entirely, as some will argue. In some instances those who used to be conservatives in the past are now worse than outcasts. For example, to have a romantic relationship with your neighbour's spouse was once considered a major sin but now people do it with pride and impunity. In the past if you came from a dysfunctional family background, people would hardly allow you to marry their loved ones, ironically now it is quite the opposite. As long as you have money, even if you have earned it through illegitimate means, no one cares. If you can obtain a passport in the West, you can get away with anything. The power has effectively shifted from parents to handouts from overseas, which caused many people to abandon farming in the field.

Such inactivity in society has significantly contributed to increased diabetes and heart disease in the communities. In the 60s, 90% of our food consumption was dependent on local farmers and now 60% of our food consumption is coming from overseas. Those living below the poverty line of $1 a day are mainly relying on imported food, yet 95% of fertile land is empty, with fantastic weather all year around. You cannot blame that on the IMF and the World Bank. Instead you can put the blame on people who are lazy and inactive. As a result, Chinese people have now started to slowly buy land in East Africa and what guarantee do we have that China and Russia will not use property investment initiative as a weapon and re-conquer Africa again with the pretext of capital investment? Not long ago the United Kingdom introduced a strict property law in order to deter foreigners from buying property in London and in 2018, New Zealand has also introduced a home ownership law in order to curb foreign property ownership in the country. Africa would need to introduce similar property laws in order to prevent another invasion from happening!

Another issue is that scholars in Africa believe that antisocial behaviour among youths has worsened after our interaction with tourists from the West. However, this may be mere speculation, because they have never provided genuine evidence to support their claim. Even though sex tourism is popular throughout the world, and certainly in Africa, tourists who are seeking such pleasure would usually mingle with like-minded men and women who are looking for similar opportunities. When they travel to visit towns and villages often they travel in groups with tour guides. An individual tourist rarely interacts alone with villagers. It occasionally occurs, but the opportunity for paedophilia or other forms of antisocial behaviour is quite slim. Paradoxically antisocial behaviour has been exacerbated by blockbuster films made in Hollywood and shown in Africa. Additionally it can be attributed to unscrupulous migrants who are returning from the West with a bad attitude.

In the West

As John Major would suggest "we have to look particularly at our relationship with the ethnic minorities, we need to acknowledge the fact we have a pretty substantial underclass and there are parts of our country where we have people who have not worked for two generations and whose children do not expect to work." I couldn't agree more. For example in the UK had the Conservative Party played its cards well, instead of 16%, the majority of people in ethnic minorities would have voted for the Tories, because they are conservatives from former colonies. When they arrive in the UK as migrants looking for labour, many either lack high education or are ill-equipped to climb the social ladder, hence they are stuck in a third world industry.

The third world industry

Let me put this into perspective for you. Please note when I say 'informal economy' I mean the black market and when I say 'third world industry' I mean manual labour. Since they started arriving in the 60s, Africans have immensely contributed to every aspect of Western society. However, the majority of them are working in the third world industries for a living and this includes: cleaning, hospitality, security, construction work, care work, astrology work and delivery work. 60% or more are in this category, compared to only 24% who are holding down a job that you would consider to be working class, i.e. nurses, teachers, musicians, office workers and small business owners. Only 10% are doctors, lawyers, police officers, teachers, sports stars and bankers; these professions can be considered as middle class jobs. Only 6% 'work' in the informal economy: the people who are earning their living through illegal means, such as drugs and theft. Based on these analyses, most Africans are trending in the working and middle class categories and not in the Western concept of upper class.

Inadequate wages in the third world industries, and financial pressure from overseas, is precisely why a high proportion of Africans who are conservatives and land owners back home cannot afford to buy their own property in the West. 90% of them are either lodging in council houses or renting from private landlords. They are usually perceived as lower casts and third class citizens. Such a dilemma puts extra pressure on the relationship between spouses, hence the divorce rate is rapidly increasing. Consequently, the crime rate is higher among the youths who came from these broken homes. Greedy parents who often demand money from their sons and daughters has occasionally contributed to divorce in the West.

And in the end, it is the children who pay the ultimate price for that, because often a single parent would struggle to discipline children effectively. The way we eat and socialise is also another challenge. You would recognise that instead of socialising outside the home most Africans enjoy visiting the homes of their families and friends. A majority cannot afford to eat out, so they frequently cook dinner for their families and guests. Due to our insatiable need for a party, as well as our strong desire for spicy food, often neighbours will complained about the noise and a strong smell in the house. Shortcomings such as these have greatly undermined the social cohesion between blacks and non-blacks.

Finally, most people are of the view that the entitlement to claim benefits and a council house is a privilege, but nothing is further from the truth. To work hard and earn your living through legitimate means and become financially independent does not only enhance your social status, but it's a moral obligation for everyone to contribute to society. You shouldn't claim the benefit if you don't need to. And yet some stupid people always argue that a benefit is a rebate of the wealth that has been looted by colonial masters in the past. It's a pity to think like that. Furthermore when you are lodging in a council house, even if you have the right to buy it at some stage, you cannot remove the taboo which is always associated with the council estate. To have status in society is quite expensive. You will only get there when you stop wasting time and you start investing to build the future.

The period of wealth creation – the future, 2035 to 2060

Political atmosphere

From 1860 to date, except the period of independence, there has been no significant economic or political progress in Africa. Without a change of course, people will continue to label Africans as ignorant, violent, corrupt and sick people. Taking into account all that I have discussed so far, you will realise that the prevailing situation in the continent is largely man-made. It has been manufactured elsewhere and then introduced to Africa. For example, when you see a charity advertising malnourished children in Africa on TV, then you compare that image to the condition of African migrants in European ghettoes, you will get the impression that all Africans are sick people.

The mainstream media will often conflate conflicts in Africa and the Caribbean with gangs and knife crime in the West, just to give people the impression that black people are violent. And when you blame lack of skills for black youth unemployment in the West and then you compare that to desperate youths from African crossing the Mediterranean Sea in their thousands to reach Europe for green pasture, it is a perfect match to feel that all these people are just a bunch of losers. Media politics and other factors have created a negative perception about black people in general. You must understand that non-blacks don't hate black skin per se, but they hate what is associated with blackness. And if we can collectively work on this together and improve our conditions, our skin colour will never hinder our progress.

Does our failure lie only in corruption and bad leadership?

Not really! Our failure lies in disunity, foreign debt and foreign interference.

For instance, in Africa, corruption in all forms counts for less than 10% of its total combined GDP. Some say Africa loses at least $148 billion per annum to corruption. Compare that to our combined GDP of $2.58 trillion - it's quite a tiny amount. Nevertheless even if we lose 1%, it's 1% too much!

It's estimated that in Africa there are approximately three thousand tribes who speak over two thousand different languages. Hence the multiparty system is based on tribal lines. Each party leader has a tribe, and without tribal loyalty they cannot survive politically and win an election. When they come to power, the main priority for them is to serve their tribes and party loyalists first. Consequently, that creates tribal hegemony, nepotism and corruption. In such a volatile environment, even if corruption is a pandemic as some would claim, it's harder to tackle it because people from other ethnic groups would not like to see the another tribe take credit for good leadership, hence they will conspire against you and sabotage your efforts.

Foreign aid and foreign debt is the roadblock to progress. The US economist Mr. Walt Whitman Rostow, masterminded the US foreign aid policy in relation to aid in Africa and its modernization process in a document he called "African Economies: Lessons of History" which is the blueprint for economic exploitation in the continent. The US hasn't use aid only as an economic weapon against Africa but it also used it as a political weapon. You may recall that on the 22nd December 2017 when the US tabled a motion at the UN to declare Jerusalem as the capital of Israel, 128 countries including The Gambia voted against it. Then the former US ambassador to the UN Nikki Haley openly threatened the countries who voted against it while she referenced the aid that US is giving to those countries; and finally she labelled them as betrayals.

The Guardian newspaper has reported that in 2015, Africa received $162 billion in overseas remittance and foreign loans. But in the same year, Africa exported £203 billion. That means that she provided $41 billion more than what she received from overseas. The same year she received $31 billion from overseas loans but she paid $18 billion, more than half of that $31 billion loan, in debt interest with the level of debt rising rapidly. Currently foreign debt stands at 60% of its GDP ratio. Other sources claimed that the annual revenue of the Shell oil company in Nigeria alone is between $158 to 165 billion. The minerals in the Congo are estimated to be around $24 trillion, while South Africa stood at $2.5 trillion. And every year countries which use the CFA Franc in Africa would deposit $500 billion as guarantees to the French central bank. If these resources and many others were properly managed, it's more than enough to sustain 1.3 billion people living in the continent. The only winners from corruption in Africa are banks in tax havens.

What is the solution?

Rostow's book "The Stages of Economic Growth" is not the solution, and racism and hostility against non-blacks as suggested by Malcolm X is not the solution. The Islamic state is not the solution, nor a Westminster type of democracy. The best way forward for Africa is A.T.O.P. - All Tribes One Party. Perhaps it would take another essay to spell this out in greater detail and how it would work effectively. As you are aware, to bring all tribes under one banner would be profoundly challenging but not impossible. Last year I asked a prominent politician to propose four policies, one in defence, one in economy, one in foreign policy and one in agriculture, which are different from the polices of other parties. It appeared as if I had asked him to reveal his personal identification numbers. He couldn't come up with anything, and then he laughed off my question. The majority of them are like that: they don't have any distinct plan. ATOP is the only way forward.

In the West

In 1964 when Kwame Nkrumah declared Ghana as a one party state, the unity among different tribes was quite central to his argument. Also in the late 80s, the former president of Kenya, Daniel arap Moi was extremely reluctant to allow a multi-party system in his country, due to fear of tribal conflict. In the early 90s, the former president of Rwanda, Juvénal Habyarimana, expressed similar concerns before he was killed in a plane crash which triggered the 1994 genocide. The disunity and division which a multi-party system could cause was a genuine concern for many in Africa since independence, but often this falls on deaf ears in the West.

Some practical examples

The United Kingdom has over 66 million people. Despite that there are only four main political 'tribes' based on social and economical ideologies: Conservative, Labour, Liberal Democrats and the Scottish National Party. The Gambia has a population of two million people, but it has more than twelve different political parties based on tribal lines. Additionally, there are only two main political parties in France (Republican and Socialist) and it has a population of almost 67 million people. By stark contrast, Senegal with a population of only 16 million people has more than twenty four different political parties based on tribal lines. Amazingly the number of political parties in the EU, with a population of 742 million, is much less than the number of political parties in Kenya, with a population of 52 million people. They have over two hundred different political parties, again not based on ideology, but instead on tribal hegemony.

The US, with a population of more than 300 million has only two main political parties. China, with the population of over one billion people, has only one. You can see that the fewer political parties you have in the country, the more unity with development and prosperity there is. The economic and social progress in Botswana, Rwanda, Singapore, Iran and Mauritius is a result of one party domination.

In addition to this, in the United Kingdom and the United States, people who serve in government are usually elevated with honour to serve their countries in different capacities. Some would be promoted to serve in the House of Lords and other would serve on various committees which advise policy makers in certain areas. Also there is a strong structure in the country which often monitors and advises the government, such as the Royal Family, the Royal Society and the Privy Council. Surely those men and women are not infallible but thanks to their experience they have contributed greatly to create strong institutions in the country.

However, due to foreign interference, that is not the case in Africa. Every new government has to start governing from scratch, with little or no experience, because hundreds of experienced people who served in the previous government with a wealth of knowledge would either be labelled as criminals and thieves, or have been given lengthy prison sentences, been sent to rot in exile or have been killed. How could anyone build strong institutions in such a brutal atmosphere? In 2008, $700 billion was mis-managed by a handful of bankers in developed countries and it caused an economic crisis throughout the world, but no one even spent a single night in a cell for such a crime, let alone a prison. If that is not a lesson for Africa, then I don't know what else will be.

You may wonder what the solutions are. The solution lies in the diaspora. Before the year 2060, Africans living in the diaspora will rescue the continent, perhaps through cultural nationalism! I will explain how.

The period of wealth reaction

You may noticed nowadays in developed countries, immigration is the biggest problem. Brexit and Trump's presidency are the clear manifestations of this. It's common now during a family feud that people will make a strong remark like "You have been living in the West for so many years and what have you achieved?" This kind of condescending remark has now begun to cause embarrassment for many people in society. It implies that after all sending all your money back home is not an achievement. Thus most people have now started soul–searching and they have started to create businesses. Hence the primary objective for most Africans living in the diaspora is no longer about status, or sending money to support their love ones through MoneyGram or Western Union, rather it's all about wealth creation.

And you will appreciate the fact that although the majority of these people are working in third world industries, they wouldn't go back home to work as physical labourers or farming in the fields like their grandfathers. Instead they will return as business owners and professionals in various fields, in pursuit of wealth creation and seeking power for glory. They will add extra demand for position and properties which could encourage people to compete more over political influence and social status. The biggest advantages for those in the diaspora are:

1. They have being living and working in the West for many years, thus most have an idea of what it takes to run the economy.

2. Communication between them is quite simple and easy, because people who speak English can share ideas without any language barriers.

3. Africans living in the West are quite relaxed about tribalism, and as you know tribalism is a major obstacle in the continent. Consequently, they could easily unite and quickly build the country together. Therefore, the next scramble for Africa before 2060 is not going to be between different white groups competing to control the land and its people, but instead it's going to be the descendants of Africans living in the diaspora.

1 will give you one small example. In 2016, Gambians living in the diaspora regardless of their tribal affiliation have come together in solidarity with the opposition coalition back home to dislodge President Jammeh from power, and they succeeded. A Gambian journalist based in Raleigh, North Carolina, Mr. Pa Nderry M'bai, was quite

instrumental in this. He created an online radio station called the Freedom Newspaper which became a platform for Gambians in the diaspora. It gave people a chance to share their views and they also used it as opportunity to express their individual frustration concerning the current affairs of the country. Later along the way it became a forum for people with enthusiasm to empower political dissidents who were scattered across Africa and elsewhere. Eventually it encouraged whistle blowers to come forward and reveal sensitive information in relation to the human rights abuses and financial embezzlement which was taking place in the country at the time.

It has galvanised people to emulate Mr. M'bai's model. As a result, Gambians have created more online radio stations in the diaspora, and the diaspora has become a battleground for political parties in the Gambia. Almost every major political party in the country has its representative in the diaspora. Some are even demanding the right for people in the diaspora to vote, while others have suggested that people in the diaspora need their own electoral constituency with a member of parliament who will represent them in the chamber. Amazingly such political patronage has now become part of the norm in Africa. In the absence of music and social ceremonies, Africans in the diaspora would come together in their thousands to raise millions of dollars, not for charities or music festivals, but to sincerely sponsor political agendas back home.

I am conscious of three challenges which could arise from my theory. One is easier to solve while the others are more difficult.

The first challenge, which is easy to solve, is that if you are a dual citizen you cannot be presidential candidate in most African countries! But here is the solution: you should bear in mind that when a revolution is about to take place, in order for it to be successful you can always bend the rules to suit the environment by any means necessary.

The second challenge is that Africa is not like China or India: it has 54 different countries which have been colonised by different countries in the West. Additionally, she has more than three thousand different ethnic groups who speak multiple languages. How do you solve these problem? Again here is the solution: these challenges were deep-rooted long before the independence struggle began. But Africans emulate each other. One country after another became independent. In order to mitigate this second challenge, once again history would have to repeat itself.

And the final challenge is that the Arab Spring, which was aimed to restore democracy in the Middle East, has failed spectacularly, chiefly because people who spearheaded the revolution haven't actually considered that a Westminster type of democracy wouldn't work, simply because it isn't compatible with Arab culture. And as result the aftermath in each country is a disaster. It's either one form of dictatorship replaced by another, or an armed conflict is currently taking place between different militia groups.

And I have argued that equally a Westminster type of democracy isn't convenient for Africa simply because tribalism would often undermine your strength and frustrate your efforts. Then what are the remedies to this? The solution is the Middle Path!

If you thoroughly study people who create dynasties, you will discovered that the empire builders would often take the middle part to build their empires. For instance, China had a philosophy based on Confucius for centuries. In addition to that, they took the middle part to study the philosophies of the US and Europe, and then they borrowed ideas from the right and the left in order to build their philosophy in the middle. The Iranians developed a similar strategy; they stood in the middle and borrowed ideas from the West and the East to build their empire. Since the advent of democracy in Europe, different countries experimented different types of democracy in order to suit their environment. Some are direct democracy, while others are representative democracy. But more often than not, each country would stand in the middle and take ideas from the right and the left. The United Kingdom created its empire because she took some ideas from Aristotle, John Locke, and Thomas Hobbes on the left and then others from the church on the right. Other countries in Europe have also adopted a similar approach in the terms of governance.

Even though there is no popular philosophy in Africa like Aristotle and Confucius, Africa should stay in the middle part, and study the philosophy and opinions of Marcus Garvey, and it should borrow ideas from the West and East in order to create its own super-power. However, the proponent of a Westminster type of democracy would often argue that the conditions for black people in the US and Caribbean hasn't been much different to that of the conditions for black people in Africa in the 1940s and 60s. Thus, if Mr. Garvey's philosophy would have worked elsewhere, as claimed by his supporters, then why it hasn't work first in the US, and the Caribbean, and elevated black people from poverty and mistreatment? Nevertheless it will work in Africa when the time is right.

The religious situation

Fake news and political hooliganism will be the biggest trouble for this decade. Unless diaspora Africans could create the middle part sooner then 2035, the struggle to control the continent between the left wing social democrats (who are pressing for a Westminster type of democracy) and the right wing Salafis (who want to introduce an Islamic state) will continue. The latter is capable of waging armed struggle against the people. Both of them have powerful allies overseas. The adherents of social democracy have studied in the West and the followers of the Salafi creed have studied in the East, and each wouldn't hesitate to sacrifice lives for their cause.

You may recalled that Sufi Islam thrived in Africa primarily because from the start it has encompassed certain indigenous beliefs such as seeking blessings from the dead ancestors and incantations. Equally, the success of Christian evangelists in Africa has been attributed to encompassing indigenous beliefs. But orthodox Salafis reckon that to practise such a belief is a heresy.

It was a missed opportunity for those who came from a Sufi background, like marabouts, to build schools and mosques when they have financial muscle in the West. They could have done better in this area but they haven't. In fact in Europe some of them have brutally failed to introduce proper discipline and pro-social behaviour of their children. But again they failed in that area too, hence the Salafis took their power base.

Education

From 2035 to 2060, Africa is poised to achieve great things but to ensure that happens first it needs to pave the way for educational reforms. The curriculum should include studies of the philosophy of Marcus Garvey, the ideas of Check anta Diop and the works of Kwame Nkrumah. There is a need for the development of African literature based on the middle part. People should realised that blockbuster films are dangerous for kids. Instead they should be encouraged to read. Due to the bad influence of films, some children would grow up thinking that to smuggle drugs and deceive people is the only way to make fast money and become rich.

For example in the 60s and 70s, the content of Indian films was dominated by astrology and black magic, which hugely projected Indians as uneducated and backward-thinking people. When they to come to realise that such content wasn't helpful to India's image, they changed the game. In order to project a more positive image of India, the content of Bollywood films is mainly about family matters and business transactions, and they have become quite popular in Africa and the Middle East. Nollywood in Nigeria hasn't made enough progress: it is lagging behind in that area. Mostly the content of its films is all about cheating and betrayal. Often on the screen you see high maintenance women seducing men for money. They could have included more educational material in their content.

Hence, in reality teenagers who can not even read or write properly will borrow romantic scraps from Nigerian films and then use that as a honey trap to seduce men who are perceived to be aspirant sugar daddies. It's a familiar territory for many. Film censorship maybe needed in certain areas to ensure that children are safe both offline and online. You may recall that until the 1950s, books and films were heavily censored in the West and currently Harry Potter and other literature which is related to magic and superstition is not allowed in the Gulf countries.

The family and the economy

A difference between Africans in the diaspora and the colonial masters was that the latter were aristocrats in Europe and they have remained such in Africa throughout the colonial period. The former were conservatives in Africa but due to their conditions in the West they remained third class citizens. The second disadvantage for Africans is that they tend to put more emphasis on entertainment than education and they don't read as much as they need to, otherwise they could have improved their situation much more quickly. The average African man in the West would spend at least $260 per annum on haircuts just to look smart, but he wouldn't spend $10 on a book in order to be more intelligent. Equally most women would spend eight hours every day in hair salons to make other women feel good but she wouldn't spend two hours to please her children and read them books. We are too eager to take care of our head, but we don't nourish our brain.

The amount of music and films that some people have accumulated in their homes is incredible. If they could convert that into books and other learning material, it would make a huge difference to many. But the saddest thing of all is that African children in the diaspora don't know much about the continent and its people, except what has been frequently projected in the mainstream media, which is far from reality. The knowledge that people of the US have about Africa is much more than the children of the Caribbean know about Africa, thanks to the US Peace Corps program.

In conclusion, people need to change attitudes and mindsets. It's hard to imagine that a president who managed to secure more foreign aid could be much popular than a president who managed to improve the education system. It is rather unfortunate that the majority of our intellectuals hold the view that corruption and bad leadership are the only problem that we have. Strangely, they haven't got a clue that corruption is only 10% of our problem. If corruption is the only thing that we should be worried about, then certainly we don't actually have anything to worry about. Above all, whatever we may achieve in future, it will not be sustainable if we don't have an effective system to defend it.

In life, whether it's about your health or your finances, in the absence of a proper defence system, you are destined to fail. In my opinion, the best weapon for war is yet to be found. Africa shouldn't fall behind in the search for one. Without efficient defence systems, North Korea and Israel would have been annihilated a long time ago. Iraq and Libya are destroyed because they lack such sophisticated defence systems.

A few years ago, I had a weird conversation with one senior officer in the army from a certain country in Africa and I asked him this: how many laboratories do you have in army camps? And he said "Zero. We don't have any. We are relying on such and such a country for supplies." I was shocked to the core. And if he is right about that while our competitors are building biological weapons, drones and bombs after many decades of independence in Africa, that would be extremely foolish; because in any business, it cannot get worse than to rely on your competitors for support.

9 7 9 8 7 1 0 8 1 4 7 0 3